REBOOT
YOUR LIFE

A Journal for Inspiration

"Writing is a process, a journey into memory and the soul."
—Isabel Allende

1

ISBN: 1482755262
ISBN 13: 9781482755268

In these pages, we invite you to write about your life and your life dreams. It can be a chronicle of daily life, ponderings, stories, ambitions, sadness and joy, change, dreams of the future. It can be absolutely anything you want.

We call the journal *Reboot Your Life* because of our book by that name. It's about stepping back from the often stressful and all-consuming daily routine to breathe, to find space. Or to start a new life chapter. We use the book and this journal in our Reboot Your Life workshops.

Journaling, which is itself a break for oneself, can be a way of finding space and time to think. There's no set formula. Those who journal know that such writing is a time of personal reflection and a superb way to identify answers already within you but that need to surface and be defined.

As you write in this journal, we hope you will be inspired by the quotes that greet you along the journey. They speak to so many human issues, emotions, and phases of life's path: overcoming self doubt and time for self, visioning, planning, transition, learning and experiencing, persistence and what lasts. The wisdom in these quotes, by men and women across the centuries and around the world, will speak to everyone uniquely as your own thoughts, memories, and dreams flow onto the pages.

Use this journal any way you wish. We just hope you are comfortable and inspired to write your own story – on these pages and in life.

Warmest wishes,

Catherine Allen
Nancy Bearg
Rita Foley
Jaye Smith

Whatever you can do, or dream you can, begin it.
Boldness has genius, power and magic in it. Begin it now.
-Johann Wolfgang von Goethe

You must do the thing you think you cannot do.
    – Eleanor Roosevelt

I always knew that one day I would take this road, but yesterday, I did not know today would be the day.

— Nagarjuna

And the day came when the risk it took to remain tight
inside the bud was more painful than the risk it
took to blossom.

— Anais Nin

It is never too late to become what you might have been.
– George Eliot

I believe that one of life's greatest risks is never
daring to risk.
— Oprah Winfrey

Aerodynamically, the bumble bee shouldn't be able to fly, but the bumble bee doesn't know it so it goes

on flying anyway.

— Mary Kay Ash

You are the storyteller of your own life and you can create your own legend, or not.

— Isabel Allende

Yet it is in our idleness, in our dreams, that the submerged truth sometimes comes to the top.

— Virginia Woolf

We don't receive wisdom; we must discover it for ourselves after a journey that no one can take for us or spare us.

— Marcel Proust

You must first be who you really are, then do what you
need to do, in order to have what you want.

— Margaret Young

What we achieve inwardly will change outer reality.
— Otto Rank

Learn to get in touch with the silence within yourself and
know that everything in this life has a purpose.
— Elisabeth Kübler-Ross

He who knows others is wise. He who knows
himself is enlightened.

– Lao-Tzu

There is nothing like a dream to create the future.
- Victor Hugo

Have the courage to follow your heart and intuition. They somehow already know what you truly want to become.
- Steve Jobs

Wheresoever you go, go with all your heart.
– Confucius

Far away there in the sunshine are my highest aspirations.
I may not reach them, but I can look up and see their
beauty, believe in them, and try to follow where they lead.
– Louisa May Alcott

Let yourself be silently drawn by the strange pull of what you really love.

— Rumi

Without leaps of imagination, or dreaming, we lose the excitement of possibilities. Dreaming, after all, is a form of planning.
– Gloria Steinem

The man who insists upon seeing with perfect clearness
before he decides, never decides.

– Henri-Frédéric Amiel

My favorite thing is to go where I've never been.
                    – Diane Arbus

A pessimist sees the difficulty in every opportunity; an optimist sees the opportunity in every difficulty.
- Winston Churchill

When choosing between two evils, I always like to try the one I've never tried before.

– Mae West

It is better to look ahead and prepare than to look back and regret.

-Jackie Joyner-Kersee

Out of clutter find simplicity.
- Albert Einstein

The bad news is time flies. The good news is
you're the pilot.
– Michael Altshuler

Twenty years from now you will be more disappointed by the things that you didn't do than by the ones you did do. So throw off the bowlines. Sail away from the safe harbor. Catch the trade winds in your sails.

Explore. Dream. Discover.

– Mark Twain

Chance is always powerful. Let your hook be always cast;
in the pool where you least expect it, there will be a fish.

— Ovid

Go confidently in the directions of your dreams! Live the life you imagined. As you simplify your life, the laws of the universe will be simpler.

- Henry David Thoreau

All endings are also beginnings. We just don't know it at the time.
- Mitch Albom

First it begins inside your heart. Something moves. Then opens. Then frees itself. And now, you feel a rhythm breaking its long silence. This is going to be good.

– Monique Duval

Life is not a having and a getting but a being
and a becoming.
— Matthew Arnold

Be not afraid of going slowly; be afraid only
of standing still.
– Chinese Proverb

True life is lived when tiny changes occur.
- Leo Tolstoy

One does not discover new lands without consenting to lose sight of the shore for a very long time.

- Andre Gide

Miracles start to happen when you give as much energy to your dreams as you do to your fears.

— Richard Wilkins

Sometimes we stare so long at a door that is closing that we see too late the one that is open.

- Alexander Graham Bell

There are only two mistakes one can make along the road
to truth: not going all the way, and not starting.
— Buddha

Write it on your heart that every day is the best
day in the year.
-Ralph Waldo Emerson

To accomplish great things, we must not only act, but also dream; not only plan, but also believe.

– Anatole France

Mistakes are part of the dues one pays for a full life.
_ Sophia Loren

Knowledge is learning something every day. Wisdom is letting go of something every day.

– Zen Proverb

You will do foolish things, but do them with enthusiasm.
– Colette

Promise me you'll always remember: You're braver than you believe, and stronger than you seem, and smarter than you think.

– Christopher Robin to Pooh (by A. A. Milne)

If you obey all the rules, you miss all the fun.
- Katherine Hepburn

This day will never come again.
- Thomas Merton

A self that goes on changing is a self that goes on living.
- Virginia Woolf

Begin at once to live, and count each separate day
as a separate life.
— Seneca

You may be disappointed if you fail, but you are doomed
if you don't try.
– Beverly Sills

Leap and the net will appear.
—John Burroughs

If you lose hope, somehow you lose the vitality that keeps life moving, you lose that courage to be, that quality that helps you go on in spite of all. And so today I still have a dream.

– Martin Luther King, Jr.

Made in the USA
San Bernardino, CA
24 February 2014